dabblelab

CREATIVE CRAFTS

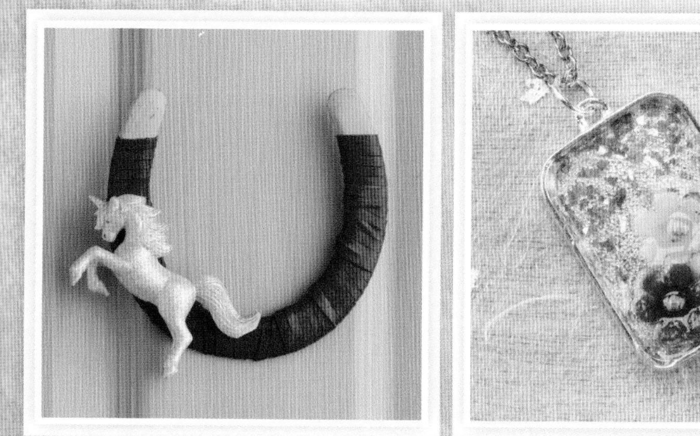

# Bought in BULK

## Projects for Surplus Supplies

Mari Bolte

Raintree is an imprint of Capstone Global Library Limited, a company incorporated in England and Wales having its registered office at 264 Banbury Road, Oxford, OX2 7DY – Registered company number: 6695582

www.raintree.co.uk
myorders@raintree.co.uk



Designed by Kayla Rossow
Production by Tori Abraham
Printed and bound in China.

ISBN 978 1 4747 4485 0
21 20 19 18 17
10 9 8 7 6 5 4 3 2 1

British Library Cataloguing in Publication Data
A full catalogue record for this book is available from the British Library.

Acknowledgements
All photos by Capstone Studio/Karon Dubke
Background design elements by Shutterstock
Project production by Marcy Morin, Kayla Rossow, Mari Bolte, Lori Blackwell and Sarah Schuette

# Contents

The passionate crafter can spend an entire afternoon exploring the world of crafting. But some supplies require up-front purchases that can leave you with lots of leftovers. So what do you do with metres of fabric, piles of pom-poms or billions of beads? Turn your scraps into fresh finds using new and innovative ways to use up extra art supplies.

# Pretty paper

Craft paper comes in so many colours and patterns. Don't let it go to waste! Use paper punches in fun shapes to create piles of butterflies, hearts, circle and birds. Then put them to use!

## Steps:

1. Make DIY stickers by mixing découpage glue with an equal amount of vinegar. Paint onto the back of scrapbook paper. Let dry, then repeat.
2. When you're ready to use a sticker, moisten the back of the paper with a little water. Then stick them to whatever you want!

**Tip:** These stickers are also easy to remove. Just press a damp sponge or cloth over the sticker for a few seconds. Then wipe away.

# Scrappy songbirds

Make a pretty mobile for your bedroom or creative space. All you need is ribbon, a metal ring, a needle and thread or fishing line and paper shapes.

## Steps:

1. Cut four 20-centimetre (8-inch) pieces of ribbon. Tie the ribbon to a metal ring, and space the ribbon evenly around the ring. Knot the loose ribbon ends together.
2. Thread a needle with fishing line or light thread. String paper shapes onto the thread. Tie a knot beneath the shapes to keep them in place.
3. Continue adding paper shapes until you've reached your desired length. Then tie a final knot and cut the thread. Tie the string of decorations to the metal ring.
4. Make as many strings as desired.
5. Finish by wrapping a ribbon or cord around the ring to hide the knots.

## Variations:

- String beads onto the fishing line for some added sparkle.
- Use glitter paper to mix in a few accent pieces to the mobile.
- Pick out a variety of papers to create a visual theme. For example, use a combination of greens and browns for a camouflage theme. Throw in one or two orange pieces for variety.
- Found items – such as small toys, pieces of hardware, fishing accessories, bells or charms – make great statement pieces.

# Cool cords

Whether you buy it in suede, braided, studded, jewelled or just plain, leather cord can be a key item for DIY jewellery. However, you might find yourself with lots of leftovers!

## Steps:

1. Make a simple wrap bracelet with coloured cord and basic jewellery making hardware. Wrap the cord around your wrist as many times as you want and then cut the cord so the ends meet.
2. Dab some craft glue onto one end of the cord and insert the cord into an end cap. Repeat on the other end. Let the glue dry completely. Then have an adult help you attach a lobster clasp to the end caps.

## Variations:

- String beads onto the cord before adding the end caps.
- Braid several strands of cord together. Use larger end caps to finish the bracelet.
- Make a necklace instead of a bracelet. Add a locket or charm, or trim the cord short to make a choker necklace.

# Wide wrist

## Steps:

1. Cut a piece of leather or thick suede about 2.5 centimetres (1 in) wide. The leather should go around your wrist, with the edges touching each other. Have an adult use a hole punch or awl to make holes every 2.5 centimetres in the leather.
2. Use one, two or three strands of cord to weave in and out of the holes. Experiment with patterns, overlapping your laces, threading them in different directions or using contrasting colours.
3. When your bracelet is to your liking, tie the ends of the cords together to close your bracelet.

**Tip:** You can also add snap fasteners to your bracelet. Cut the leather a little longer so the edges overlap. Then have an adult use a setting tool and a hammer to add buttons or snaps.

## Variations:

- You can also cover things in leather! Wrap an old horseshoe with suede leather. Keep the suede tight as you wrap and use glue to keep the suede in place. Glue on a toy horse or unicorn for extra luck!

♥ TRY IT!

# Really resin

Casting resin can help capture bits of memories and remind you of special places or times.

## Steps:

1. Place a metal binder ring onto a piece of clear parcel tape. Carefully press the ring's edges onto the tape.
2. Press a small bead onto the tape, near the top of the binder ring. The hole should be facing up.
3. Decorate the center of the ring with glitter. Use a toothpick to press the glitter onto the tape.
4. Have an adult prepare resin according to package instructions. Pour resin into the center of the ring. Use a toothpick to spread the resin evenly. Pop any bubbles that may appear. Be careful not to pour any resin into the bead hole!
5. Let the resin cure before removing the tape. Use sandpaper to smooth out any rough edges. Thread wire or string through the bead hole to hang your piece.

## Variations:

• Use a bezel instead of the binder ring. Bezels already have holes for hanging, so you won't need the bead.

• Make coasters by pouring resin into jar lids. You can also buy resin moulds so you can make coasters (or anything else they make a mould of) and pop them out easily.

• You can cast anything in resin! Things you can find outdoors, like sand, leaves or stones are nice for a natural look. But use whatever you have a lot of! Leftover craft supplies, such as beads, charms and buttons, or ordinary objects such as coins or bits of metal work well too. Try colourful sweets and sprinkles!

**Tip:** Be sure to follow all the directions on the resin! Wear gloves and protect your clothing and work surface. Greaseproof paper is a great inexpensive way to keep resin off your table.

**Tip:** You can colour resin too! Use a little mica powder and spread it around with a toothpick while the resin is still wet.

# Billions of beads

Do you have a billion beads? Make a dent in your stash by constructing something beautiful. A large metal macramé ring, beading wire and a bunch of beads can become a dazzling suncatcher with just a few quick twists.

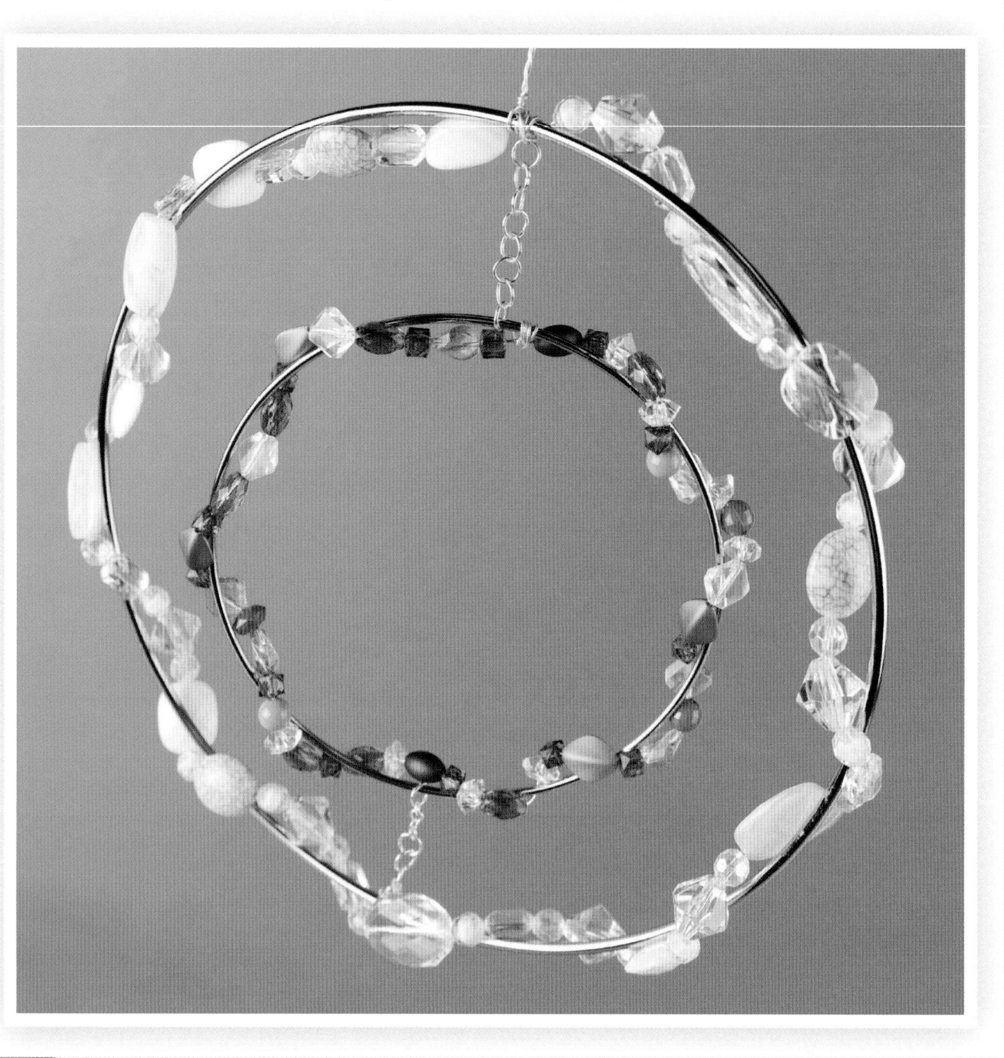

## Steps:

1. Pick out your beads and lay them in a pattern. You can buy lengths of beads that already coordinate, or make your own combination of colours and shapes.
2. String the beads onto 20 gauge beading wire. The thicker wire will hold heavier beads.
3. Wrap the beaded wires around a large macramé ring. Repeat with a smaller macramé ring.
4. Use jump rings or lengths of chain to suspend the smaller ring inside the larger ring. Attach another piece of chain from the top of the large ring, and add a hook or suction cup.

## Variations:

- Macramé rings come in a variety of sizes. Try using three rings or hanging them in one long chain instead of inside one another.

- Hang strings of beaded wire from the ring to make a wind chime. Use the resin rings on pages 10 and 11 as accent pieces.

- Try experimenting with this technique using a thin photo frame, silverware handles or even things like pens or bottles.

- Any kind of bead will work! Pony or seed beads are craft supplies that always seem to be on hand.

**Tip:** If you can't find a macramé ring, embroidery hoops or wreath forms will also work.

**Tip:** Although 20 gauge wire works well for hanging beads, you can try different wire sizes for wrapping the ring.

# It's raining rainbows

You wanted every colour but those little rubber bands add up, one bag at a time! What do you do when there's nothing left to loom?

## Steps:

1. Add a little sparkle to some basic rubber bands. Open a jump ring and string on a seed bead or two. Then add three bands. Close the jump ring.
2. Attach another beaded jump ring to the rubber bands. Then add more bands to that ring. Continue alternating rubber bands and jump rings until you have a bracelet or necklace your desired length.

## Variations:

- Use more jump rings, more beads or more rubber bands! Use four bands instead of three, or two jump rings and two rubber bands. Leave off the beads if you prefer. Or add charms instead!

# Stretchy strings

## Steps:

1. String art can be fun, but rubber bands come in more colours! Have a piece of scrap wood handy.
2. Find a design you like online and cut out your pattern. You can also use a basic stencil or even a real picture. Trim the pattern so it fits on the wood and position it how you like.
3. Have an adult help gently tap small nails around the outline of your pattern. Make sure the nails are not placed further apart than a rubber band will stretch.
4. Once your design is nailed down, gently pull off what's left of your paper pattern.
5. Colour in your design using the rubber bands. Try to keep a similar amount of tension between the rubber bands and the nails. If you run into areas where the nails are too close together to keep the band tight, give the rubber band a twist. Then continue on to the next nail. Keep banding until your entire design is coloured.

## Variation:

• Paint the wood and the heads of the nails for a little more colour.

**Tip:** Tap lightly – just enough to keep the nails secure. They should all be about the same height.

**Tip:** A crochet hook or loom hook will help when placing the bands.

# Tangled in thread

Embroidery thread is fun to collect in every colour.
Weave it, wrap it, braid it or bead it!

Make a statement bracelet in any colour you can imagine. You'll need a zip, embroidery thread and some basic jewellery making supplies. No special skills needed!

## Steps:

1. Undo the zip so you have two pieces. Wrap the half with the zip pull loosely around your wrist. Trim off the excess zip. Cut off 2.5 centimetres (1 in) of the zip from the trimmed end.
2. The other half of the zip should have tails on both ends. Cut off the tail on one end.
3. Start with the zip with the pull still attached. At the end with the pull, fold the zip fabric in half. Then tie a piece of embroidery thread around the zip.

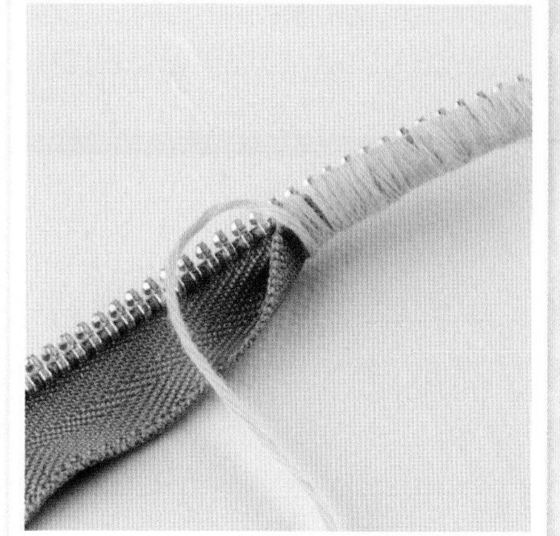

4. Begin wrapping embroidery thread around the zip. Pull it tight around the fabric and loop it between the zip's teeth. Wrap as many times as necessary to completely cover the zip's fabric. When you get to the end, tie the embroidery thread and trim off the excess.
5. Repeat step 3 with the second zip half. Use the embroidery thread to tie the end with no tail to the first zip half before repeating step 4.
6. Cross the zip halves over and under each other. Use a dot of glue to press the zip tails together. Then press the tail ends into a ribbon crimper and close shut.
7. Attach a lobster clasp to the ribbon crimper with a jump ring. Clip the lobster clasp to the hole in the zip pull to finish your bracelet

## Variation:

• Try embroidery thread instead of leather cord on the project on page 9, and vice versa here! A simple switch will change the entire look of your project.

• Dress down your bracelet by using a plastic zip instead of metal.

• Hang a charm off the zip pull from a jump ring.

**Tip:** Use a zip with large teeth. Small zips won't work for this project.

# Coated in candy

Candy melts are fun, but they also have a sell-by date. Don't let them go to waste! Or, even worse, go out of season. Who wants to eat pastel candy in October?

## What you'll need:

- apples
- sticks
- blue candy melts
- white sprinkles
- baking tray
- baking paper

## Steps:

1. Prep your apples by washing and drying the outsides well. Have an adult help you add a wooden lollipop stick to the center of each apple. Let the apples come to room temperature before dipping.
2. Melt blue candy melts according to the package's directions. Dip an apple into the candy, leaving a small space at the top uncoated. Let the excess coating drip off.
3. Spread sprinkles out on a small shallow plate. Set each apple in the sprinkles. Use a spoon to stick sprinkles onto the bottom halves of the apples.
4. Place the apples on a tray covered in baking paper and let set in the fridge until the candy coating is firm.

**Tip:** To use candy melts for drizzling or piping, place melts in a plastic ziplock bag. Fold the top of the bag over and microwave at 50% power for 30 seconds. Knead the bag. Microwave for another 15 seconds and knead again. Repeat until the candy melts are smooth and melted. Cut one corner of the bag for decorating. Make a small hole for piping or a larger one for drizzling.

## Variations:

- Get a little scary! Dip an entire apple in orange candy melts and sprinkle the top of the apple with brown sprinkles. Pipe faces or Jack-o'-lantern features on with yellow melts. Use more melts to glue on sugar eyes.
- Pipe designs directly onto the apple. Use a variety of colours or just one to keep things simple. Write peoples' names or try drawing animal faces.
- Use candy melts for painting. Use a small paintbrush (that you only use for food) or a toothbrush to paint designs onto your apples. *Starry Night* on an apple? Go for it!

**Tip:** Candy melts aren't just for apples! Dip biscuits, pretzels, marshmallows or other fruits. Invite your friends over and have a candy melts fondue party! Everyone can bring something different to dip.

# Rolls of ribbon

You can buy ribbon by the metre but the most common way to get your hands on some is by the roll. Get the most out of leftover ribbon by turning it into one of the most useful accessories ever – a bunch of bookmarks! Keep your favourites and give a few away to friends.

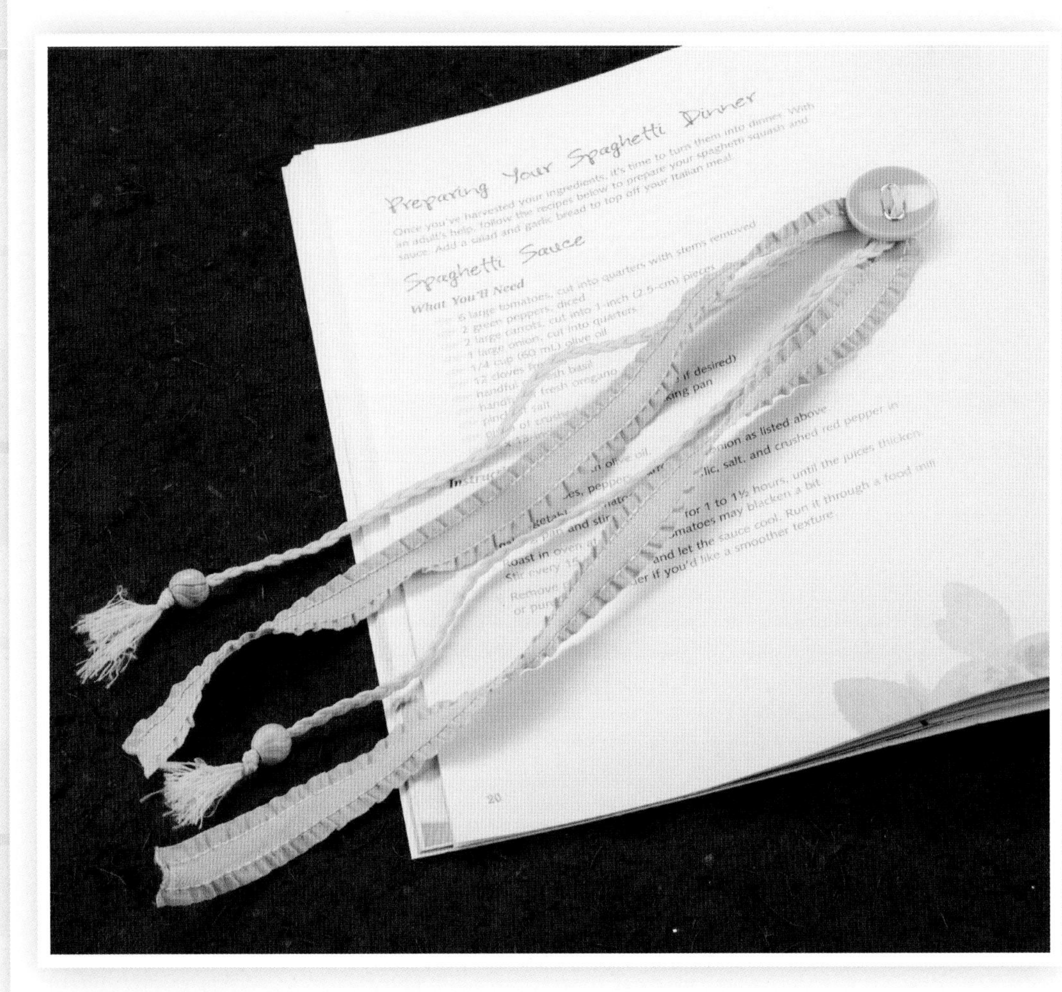


## Bookmark 1:

Find a button with two holes wide enough to run your ribbon through. Cut 46-centimetre (18-in)-long pieces of cord and ribbon. Run the ends of the cord and ribbon through the button. Thread a bead onto each end of the cord and tie a knot to keep the bead in place.

## Bookmark 2:

Cut a 25.5-centimetre (10-in)-long piece of ribbon. Dab a bit of glue onto the ends and attach ribbon ends. Crimp the ribbon ends shut. Use a jump ring to attach a charm or pendant to the ribbon ends.

**Tip:** To keep your ribbon ends from fraying, paint the ends of the ribbon with anti-fraying liquid, craft glue or clear nail polish.

## Bookmark 3:

Cut two 46-centimetre (18-in)-long pieces of ribbon and glue them together. Lay the ribbons right side up on your work surface. Glue one magnet to the top of the ribbon on one end, and another to the underside of the ribbon on the other end. Glue a charm or embellishment to the top of the ribbon so it sits directly over the magnet.

## Variation:

- To make your bookmark more adjustable, space out and glue down several magnets evenly across the top of the ribbon.

# Hot for hot glue

Turn leftover glue sticks into something you can take anywhere.

## Steps:

1. Lay baking paper out on your work surface. Measure your finger for a ring and draw a line that length onto the baking paper. Then use hot glue to create a pattern over the line. (It can be as wide as you want.)
2. Let the glue dry completely before removing it from the baking paper. Gently bend the glue into a ring. Close the ring shut with more hot glue.

## Variation:

- Colour hot glue after it's dry with spray paint, acrylic paint, nail polish or permanent markers. You can also buy coloured hot glue sticks.

## Variations:

- Cut a piece of lace or fabric in your ring measurements. Set the baking paper over the fabric and use the fabric outline as a template to make a hot glue design of the same size. Let the glue cool. Turn the glue shape over so the flat side faces you. Use fabric glue to attach the lace, face-up, to the glue shape. Let dry. Then shape the glue into a ring shape and close shut with hot glue.

- Press small gems into the glue while it's still hot.

- Paint glue shapes with découpage glue and then coat with glitter. Once the découpage glue is dry, add another coat to keep the glitter from flaking. Let it dry completely before wearing.

- You can make all sorts of hot glue jewellery! Try necklaces, bracelets or even masks. Hot glue gauntlets or a crown could make an exciting accessory to any costume. Hot glue is strong enough and flexible enough to make many types of fashion accessories.

# Stuck on duct tape

Duct tape is an emergency-situation must-have. But some might consider having lots of duct tape (and nothing to do with it) an emergency too! Don't get stuck with lots of leftovers – turn it into tons of fun instead.

## Steps:

1. To make a key ring you'll carry everywhere, cut a 25.5-centimetre (10-in) piece of duct tape. Lay it sticky-side up on your work surface.
2. Starting in the center, fold the top third in. Work slowly to avoid wrinkles and press firmly for a straight edge.
3. Fold the bottom third in. All the sticky edges should now be covered.
4. Fold your key ring in half with the crease sides in. Loop the ends through a key ring. Fold them around a key ring. Wrap a small piece of tape around the ends to hide them. Add an embellishment or sticker to the small piece of tape, if desired.

## Variations:

- Make a lanyard instead by cutting a 1-metre (3-foot)-long piece of tape. Add a lanyard hook to the key ring.
- Use a 25-millimetre (1-in) O-ring instead of a key ring to make a water bottle carrier. The O-ring will fit perfectly over a water bottle's screw cap.
- Make your duct tape fancier by adding thin strips of decorative duct tape, or add washi or glitter tape.

# Taped together

## Steps:

1. Pre-made duct tape sheets are a great shortcut to great things. Place two sheets on top of each other, decorative sides out. (Don't remove the sheets' backing.) Use strips of tape along the edges of the sheets to connect the sides and bottom of the bag.
2. Cut two 46-centimetre (18-in)-long pieces of duct tape. Follow the key fob instructions to make straps. Use more tape to attach the handles to the bag.

**Tip:** To make your own sheets of duct tape, lay a strip of tape your desired length sticky side up on your work surface. Add a second strip, overlapping it 6 millimetres (¼ in). Continue overlapping strips of tape until the sheet is as long as you need. Then add more strips of tape on top, sticky side down.

# Metres of fabric

Whether you're left with entire metres, fat quarters or just scraps, there's no need to waste fabric! Give fun prints new life with some simple steps.

1. Wrap tulle around your hand about a dozen times. Remove your hand and cut the tulle.
2. Measure and cut another piece of tulle about 10 centimetres (4 in) long. Fold it in half horizontally. Then fold it in half again.
3. Tie the small piece of tulle around the center of the wrapped tulle. You should have a bow shape, with the folds of the tulle facing out.
4. Use scissors to cut through all the folded ends of the tulle. Fluff up the tulle to make a pom-pom. Use hot glue or small headpins to attach pom-poms to the ends of pencils.

## Variations:

- Colour tulle-topped pencils with acrylic paint. Write messages with a fine-tip permanent marker, or use more paint to add decorations.
- Instead of paint, try wrapping pencils in leftover fabric or tulle. You can also découpage fabric right onto the pencils.
- Use yarn to make pom-poms instead! You'll have to wrap more (90 to 100 times instead of a dozen) but you won't have to fluff anything at the end.

**Tips:**

Choosing fabric can be an overwhelming task! Some types are easier to work with than others. Learn more about some commonly found fabrics and the best way to work with them.

- **tulle** is a lightweight, netlike fabric that can be bought by the metre or in rolls. It can sometimes be staticky. If it starts to stick to things, give it a light spray with water.
- **cotton** is woven from a natural fiber. It is affordable, comes in many colours and patterns, and works well for any craft. Pre-cut fat quarters or remnants are excellent choices when building your library of cotton fabrics.
- **denim** and **chambray** are woven fabrics. They are more durable than cotton or tulle. Sharp fabric scissors are important tools when cutting these thicker fabrics.

**Tip:** Store fabric in plastic boxes. Sort it by colour so you'll be able to find exactly what you need every time! Place smaller scraps in jars or plastic ziplock bags.

**Tip:** Rotary cutters will make trimming fabric a breeze! Armed with a cutting mat to protect your work surface and a ruler, straight edges will come out perfect every time.

# Printed with love

Make mail even more fun by sending it in fabric envelopes!

## Steps:

1. Ask an adult to help you open a regular paper envelope. Open the flaps and lay the envelope flat over your fabric. Trace the envelope over your fabric and cut it out.
2. Cover one side of the fabric with matte découpage glue. Let dry completely. Repeat with the other side. The fabric should dry stiff but flexible.
3. Smooth any corners and tidy up any crooked edges if necessary. Fold the fabric envelope edges in. Use a straight edge such as a ruler, to make sure your folds are crisp. Then use a small amount of glue to seal the edges.

**Tip:** If you want to send these through the mail, spray envelopes with a waterproof sealer to protect both your mail and the postal service's equipment. And add an extra stamp – and maybe a dab of glue!

# Scrap lights

Light up your favourite space with a source that brings some old favourites together.

## How to:

Simply tie fabric strips around a string of lights! Display the lights in your favourite reading nook or cozy craft corner.

## Variations:

- Save old clothes and worn-out blankets or bags and turn them into fabric strips instead of throwing them away. (Ask before you cut though!) You'll have fond memories every time you look at your lights.
- Try ribbon or tulle instead of regular fabric.
- Wrap your finished fabric lights around a wreath form for door décor that can be displayed year-round. Or try wrapping them around a Christmas tree.

# A purse full of pom-poms

Pom-poms are so fun – until you're left with a bagful! Luckily, pom-poms make great embellishments for anything that might need a little pop.

## How to:

Use hot glue or fabric glue to decorate simple bags with pom-poms. Cover the entire bag or just add a handful! Test out different sizes and colours of pom-poms.

## Variation:

- Use pom-poms to line bag flaps, basket edges or even flip-flop straps.

# Pom-pom garland

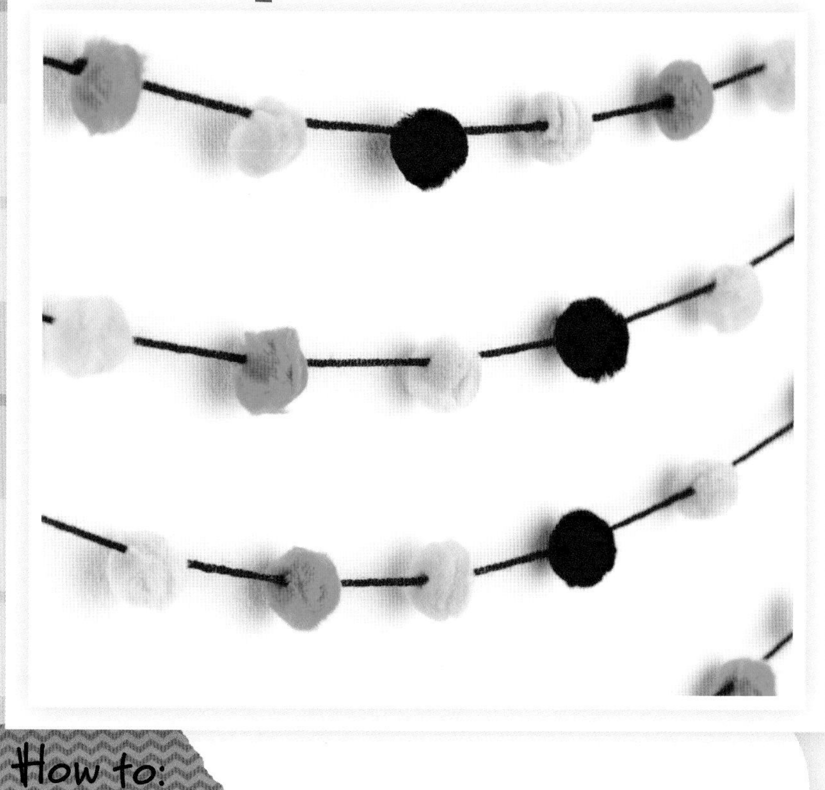

## Variations:

- Make your bookshelf stand out with these quick DIY bookends. Glue a wooden letter to a flat piece of wood. Use hot glue to cover the letter with pom-poms. Repeat to make a second bookend.
- Cover the flat piece of wood with découpage glue and then with fancy paper. Paint another layer or two of glue over the top. Then add the letter.

## How to:

With an adult's help, use an embroidery needle and yarn to string pom-poms. String them so they're closer together or space them out a little.

# Books

Junk Modelling (10 Minute Crafts), Annalees Lim (Wayland, 2016)

Recycling and Reusing (Discover Through Craft), Louise Spilsbury (Franklin Watts, 2017)

Recycling Crafts (Craft Attack!), Annalees Lim (Franklin Watts, 2014)

# Websites

**http://blog.hobbycraft.co.uk/craft-ideas/**
Packed with tips and tricks to get your creative juices flowing!

**http://www.redtedart.com/**
Fun and easy arts and crafts for every season!

**http://kidscraftroom.com/**
Inspirational art and craft ideas to enjoy throughout the year.